KT-497-743

Contents

Introduction

In this book you can learn about dinosaurs both by reading about them and by having fun with craft activities. The information in the fact boxes will tell you about the meat-eating dinosaurs and the plant-eaters, as well as related reptiles. Of course, no one has ever seen a dinosaur as humans appeared on Earth over 60 million years after the dinosaurs had died out. So all that we know about them has been gained from fossils - remains preserved in rocks.

At the end of the book is a time chart to show you when all the dinosaurs mentioned in this book lived. There is also a list of places to visit if you want to find out more.

But now you can get your fingers sticky - making dinosaurs as you read all about them.

Equipment and Materials

The projects in this book provide an introduction to the use of different art and craft media, and need little adult help. Most of the objects are made with throwaway household "junk" such as boxes, plastic bottles and containers, newspaper and fabric remnants. Natural things such as seeds, sticks, sand and stones are also used. Paints, brushes, glues and modelling materials will have to be bought, but if stored correctly will last for a long time and for many more craft activities.

In this book the following materials are used:

air-hardening clay
balloon (round)
boot polish (tan)
broom handle
brushes (for glue and paint)
buttons
canes (pencil thickness)
card (thick and thin)
cardboard boxes (two must be identical)
cardboard tubes
cellophane
cereal box
cloth (scraps)
egg-boxes
felt pieces (red, green, white, black, orange)
felt-tip pens
food colouring (green)
glue (water-based PVA, which can be used for thickening paint and as a varnish, strong glue for sticking plastic, metal or fabric)
jar (for mixing paint and paste)
lolly stick
materials from nature (sticks, twigs, leaves, stones, pine cones, seeds)
modelling materials (air-hardening clay, plasticine)

paint (powder, ready-mixed or poster paints, water-colour inks)
paper (thick cartridge paper, corrugated paper, crêpe paper, tissue paper, newspaper, sugar paper)
pencil
pipe-cleaner
plaster of Paris
plastic bottles
plasticine
rolling-pin
ruler
sand (fine, dry builders' sand)
scissors
silver foil
sponge
stapler
sticky tape and tabs (parcel tape, masking tape)
straws
string
toilet roll tubes
trays and tubs
varnish (PVA mixed with cold water)
wallpaper paste
water

Valley of the Dinosaurs

1 To make a prehistoric landscape, first put the shallow box together like this. The lid becomes the background and the base is the valley.

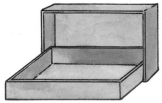

YOU WILL NEED:
- ✓ crêpe paper ✓ tissue paper ✓ glue
- ✓ cellophane ✓ plasticine ✓ straws
- ✓ shallow box with lid ✓ coloured sugar paper
- ✓ builders' sand ✓ green ink or food colouring
- ✓ natural objects (fir cones, twigs etc)
- ✓ stones and pebbles

2 Line the box with blue paper. Cut out coloured-paper mountains and volcanoes and stick them to the blue sky. The skyline should be above the rim of the box.

3 Colour some dry builders' sand green, to make it look like moss. Stir the sand while it is soaking up the colouring. Leave it to dry overnight.

WARNING: Never hold cellophane right up to your face.

4 To make a lake in the valley, lay a piece of blue paper on the base of the box and place some cellophane on top of it. Sprinkle the green sand around the edge.

5 Arrange stones and pebbles to look like mountains with caves and secret passages.

6 Giant trees and plants grow in the valley. Fir cones, twigs, beech husks and other natural objects pressed into plasticine trunks make good bushes. Make ferns by taping green tissue paper around straws planted in lumps of plasticine. Strips of crêpe paper make good creepers.

7 Mould a *Diplodocus* by rolling out a ball of plasticine and six sausage shapes for a neck, tail and legs. Press the shapes together and stand the dinosaur up. Mark eyes and mouth with a toothpick. Make lots of other dinosaurs this way and let them roam through the valley of the dinosaurs. (Don't forget that some of the reptiles were as tall as the trees.)

The Age of Dinosaurs

Dinosaurs were large reptiles. They appeared on Earth about 230 million years ago. The age of dinosaurs lasted for about 165 million years. Then they all died out. But what was the Earth like at that time?

At the beginning of the age of dinosaurs, one deep ocean covered most of the Earth (above). All the land formed one huge super-continent. So early dinosaurs could walk across the world! Later the land masses moved apart to make the continents that we know today.

Fish, amphibians and giant insects such as dragonflies existed before the dinosaurs. Large fern trees grew in swamps, and there were forests of cone-bearing trees. The first birds and small mammals appeared during the age of the dinosaur, followed later by fruit trees and flowering plants.

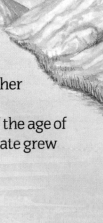

Throughout much of their time on Earth, dinosaurs probably lived in a tropical climate.

Land near the sea had mild, moist weather all year round.

Towards the end of the age of dinosaurs, the climate grew cooler and drier.

Tyrannosaurus Hobby-horse

YOU WILL NEED:
✓ large sock   ✓ pins
✓ broom handle   ✓ ruler
✓ old material and
    newspaper for stuffing
✓ white, black, orange felt
✓ glue   ✓ scissors   ✓ ribbon

1 Stuff the foot of the sock with scraps of material. Put two small balls of newspaper into the sock to make eye ridges.

2 Cut two 20 cm strips of jagged teeth and a strip of red felt 18 cm x 10 cm for the inside of the mouth.

3 Pin the mouth and teeth together before gluing them into position. Remove the pins. Add thin strips of black felt around the mouth as shown.

4 Cut two mean-looking orange felt eyes, two white dots and black pupils. Assemble the eyes like this. Stick them below the ridges. Cut two black eyebrows and stick them on top of the ridges. Add two red dots for nostrils.

5 Push the broom handle into the sock as far as the heel. Stuff newspaper firmly all around it. Tie a piece of ribbon around the sock to hold the head on. Now you can ride on *Tyrannosaurus!*

Tyrannosaurus Rex

Tyrannosaurus was the biggest meat-eating dinosaur. It was about 15 metres long and weighed between 4 - 7 tonnes. If this dinosaur was alive today, it would be able to peer into the upstairs windows of a modern house.

Tyrannosaurus fought and often killed other dinosaurs. Some scientists, however, think that it mostly fed on the bodies of dead dinosaurs. This was because it was too slow to catch its own food.

Its head was almost 2 metres long, and its long teeth had sawlike edges for tearing flesh. It had powerful claws on its hind legs, which it probably used to grip its prey. But the front legs were very small, with two small fingers on the hand, and could not even reach its mouth.

Tyrannosaurus Rex means "king tyrant lizard".

Dinosaur Footprints

1 Take a ball of clay and make a model dinosaur foot. Gently press it on a flat surface and shape three claws.

YOU WILL NEED:
✔air-hardening clay ✔plaster of Paris ✔plasticine ✔sponge ✔plastic tray ✔rolling-pin ✔sugar paper ✔ready-mix paint ✔cloth ✔lolly stick

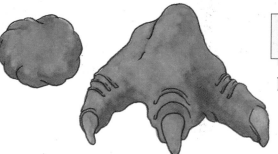

2 Make some marks with a lolly stick or your finger on the base of the foot. Leave it to harden.

3 Now make a trail of prints across the sheet of paper with your dinosaur foot. Pour some paint onto a sponge and press the foot against it. Print a trail across your paper. Wipe the foot clean if you want to use a different colour.

4 To make a cast of one footprint, roll out a lump of plasticine until it is the size of your tray. Put the plasticine on the bottom of the tray.

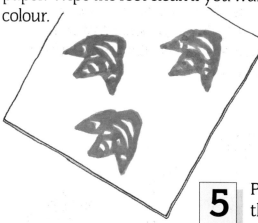

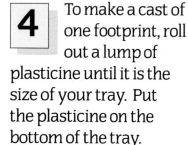

5 Press the foot firmly into the plasticine and remove it to show an imprint.

6 With an adult's help, mix the plaster of Paris in a bowl with some water. Pour the liquid plaster over the footprint in the plasticine. You can paint your dinosaur foot while you are waiting for the plaster to dry.

7 When the plaster is completely dry, carefully turn it out of the tray, peel off the plasticine and study your fossil.

Fossil prints

Imagine finding footprints that were made 150 million years ago! It seems incredible, but that is exactly what scientists have done. Dinosaurs walked over the soft ground and left footprints. Then the ground hardened into rock, leaving fossil footprints. *Iguanodon* footprints (left) have been found in many parts of Europe and Africa. Like other fossils, these have told us a lot about dinosaurs.

Several dinosaurs walked upright on their hind legs. Some, like *Tyrannosaurus*, were slow, while others, such as *Segisaurus* (right), could run fast.

Many of the long-necked plant eaters, such as *Diplodocus*, were enormous and walked on all fours. The two-footed plant-eaters had blunt hooves on their feet, like an elephant, while meat-eaters had sharp claws with which to catch and kill their prey.

Stegosaurus Disguise

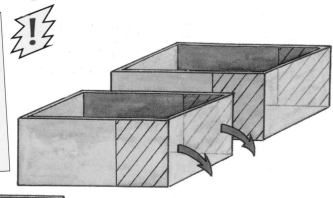

YOU WILL NEED:
- ✔ glue ✔ adhesive pads ✔ sticky tape ✔ scissors
- ✔ egg-boxes ✔ ruler ✔ pins ✔ pencil ✔ brushes
- ✔ 3 big cardboard boxes (2 must be identical)
- ✔ green cartridge and sugar paper ✔ ruler
- ✔ powder or ready-mix paint ✔ silver foil

1 Find two identical boxes big enough to fit over your head and shoulders. Ask an adult to cut away the shaded part and open out the bottom of the boxes.

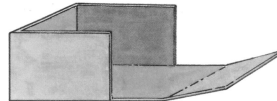

2 Slide one box inside the other and tape them together. Try on your *Stegosaurus* body. Mark the position of your eyes and ask an adult to cut out a peephole in the front.

3 For the head, glue another box on top of the dinosaur body.

4 Now decorate your disguise. Cover the boxes with green paper, or paint them with green paint thickened with PVA glue. When the paint is dry, mark the scales with black paint. Out of sugar paper, make two eyes and a mouth with teeth and stick them onto the head.

5 Cut spine plates from green cartridge paper 15 cm wide. Add a 3 cm fold. Attach the plates to the top of the head box and the body with adhesive pads under the fold. Secure them with sticky tape.

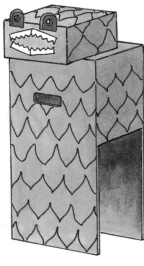

6 Cut out a long green paper tail - wide enough to fit onto the back of the dinosaur's body. Cut the egg-boxes up into single cups and paint them green. When they are dry, stick the cups onto the tail to make scales. Also add some screwed up foil and green paper as shown. For tail spikes, screw up four strips of silver foil and attach them to the end to the tail.
Glue the scaly tail to the body.
Now all you have to do is
wait for an invitation to
a dinosaur party!

Armoured Dinosaurs

Armoured plant-eaters walked on all fours. They didn't need to run away from their enemies as they could protect themselves in other ways. *Stegosaurus* ("plated lizard") was slow and clumsy. It was about 6 metres long, weighed 2 tonnes and had a brain about the size of a walnut.

It was called "plated lizard" because it had two rows of bony plates running down its back. These were probably used to control its body heat as well as providing protection from enemies. *Stegosaurus* also had four sharp spikes at the end of its tail. It used these against attacking meat-eating dinosaurs.

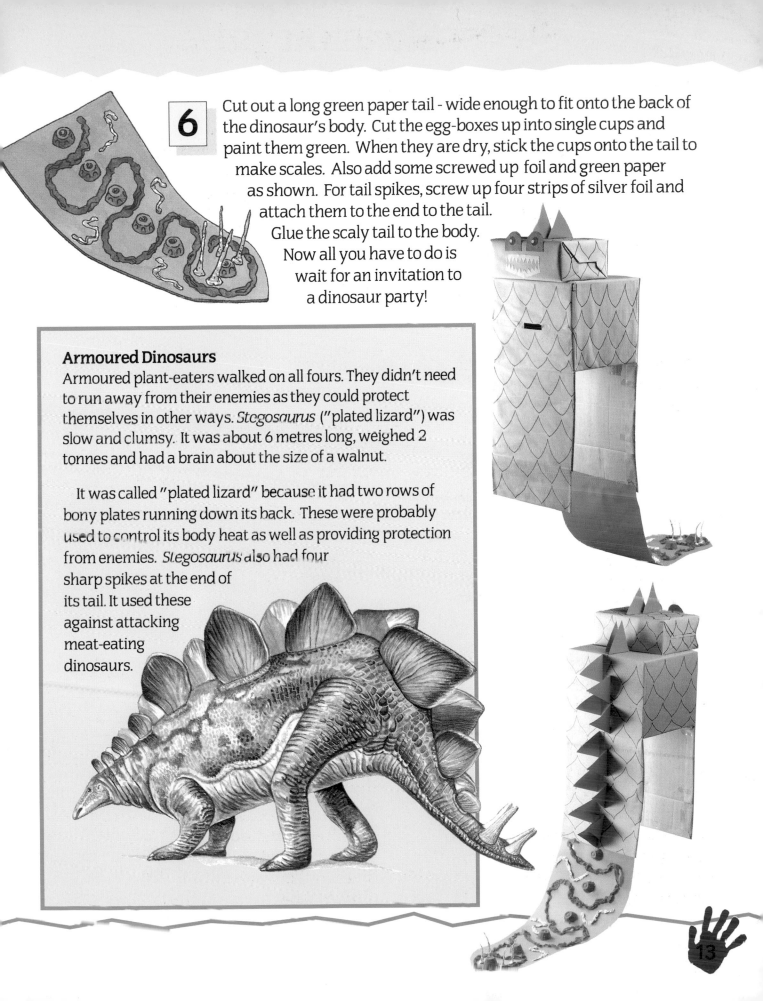

Skeleton

YOU WILL NEED:
- ✔ cardboard   ✔ straws
- ✔ fine dry sand   ✔ scissors
- ✔ PVA glue   ✔ glue brush

Be a fossil hunter and make your own dinosaur skeleton.

1 Cut up straws into different lengths for bones. Fit the straws together on a cardboard base, copying a drawing of a dinosaur skeleton.

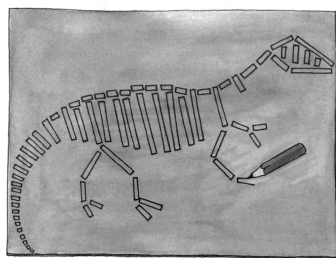

2 When you have assembled the skeleton, stick the straws down one by one. Brush each straw with PVA glue and fix it in position. Make sure that all the straws are firmly attached to the cardboard base. Wait for the glue to dry.

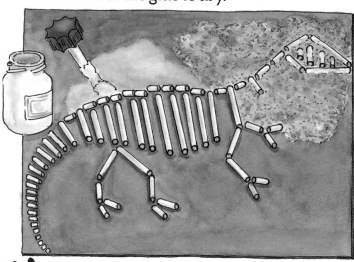

3 Now brush some glue thickly between the bones and all around the straw skeleton. Sprinkle sand over the glue. It is best to work with a small section at a time while the glue is still wet.

Dinosaur Bones

There are many skeletons of dinosaurs on display in museums. The fossil bones of a complete skeleton are wired together by experts. But it is rare for fossil bones to be tidily arranged when they are found. They are usually broken up in the rocks into small pieces. They have to be put together in the right order to make the animal recognizable.

When Gideon and Mary Mantell found dinosaur remains in 1822, they named the creature *Iguanodon* ("iguana tooth"). This was because the teeth looked like those of the South American iguana lizard.

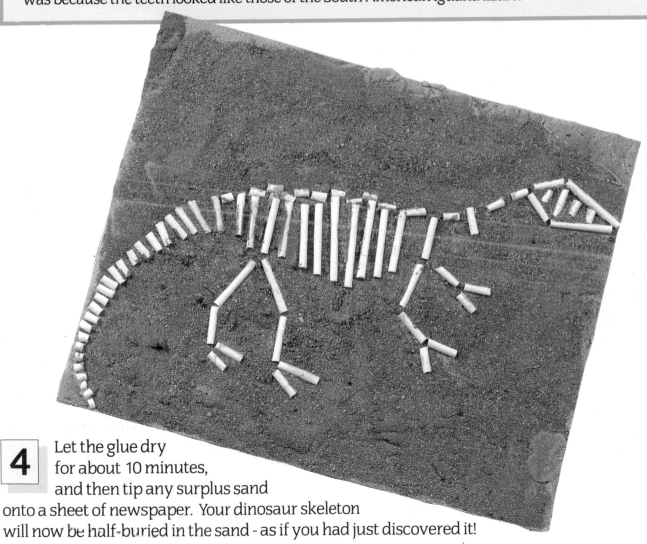

4 Let the glue dry for about 10 minutes, and then tip any surplus sand onto a sheet of newspaper. Your dinosaur skeleton will now be half-buried in the sand - as if you had just discovered it!

Flying Reptiles

YOU WILL NEED:
✓ coloured card or thick paper ✓ pipe cleaners ✓ nylon thread ✓ curtain ring ✓ glue brush ✓ glue ✓ scissors ✓ sticky tape ✓ black felt pen ✓ ruler ✓ pencil

1 To make a pet *Pteranodon* take a piece of card 10 cm x 28 cm and fold it in half lengthways.

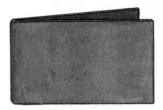

2 Copy the shape of the wing and cut it out. Don't cut the fold.

3 For the head and beak, fold a piece of card 10 cm x 6 cm in half lengthways. Copy this arrowshape and cut it out. Don't cut the fold. Draw on the eyes and the beak with black felt tip pen. Fold an 8 cm strip of card lengthways and cut out a thin tail.

4 Make the body by rolling up a sheet of paper, slightly wider than the centre of the wings, and glue it together.

5 Glue pipe-cleaner legs at one end of the tube and stick the tail inside the body. Glue on the head. Cut out a card crest and stick it as shown.

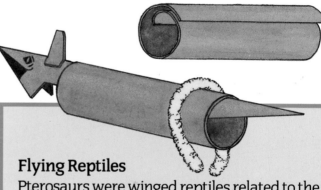

6 Open the wings and tape a curtain ring to the wing top.

Flying Reptiles

Pterosaurs were winged reptiles related to the dinosaurs. Their wings were covered with skin and were used for gliding. *Pteranodon* is one of the largest known flying animals that has ever lived. It had a wingspan of 7 metres. Scientists think that *Pteranodon* lived on high cliffs where it could take off easily. It must have been very clumsy on the ground because it had weak legs and could not fold its wings completely.

7 Now glue the wings onto the *Pteranodon's* body.

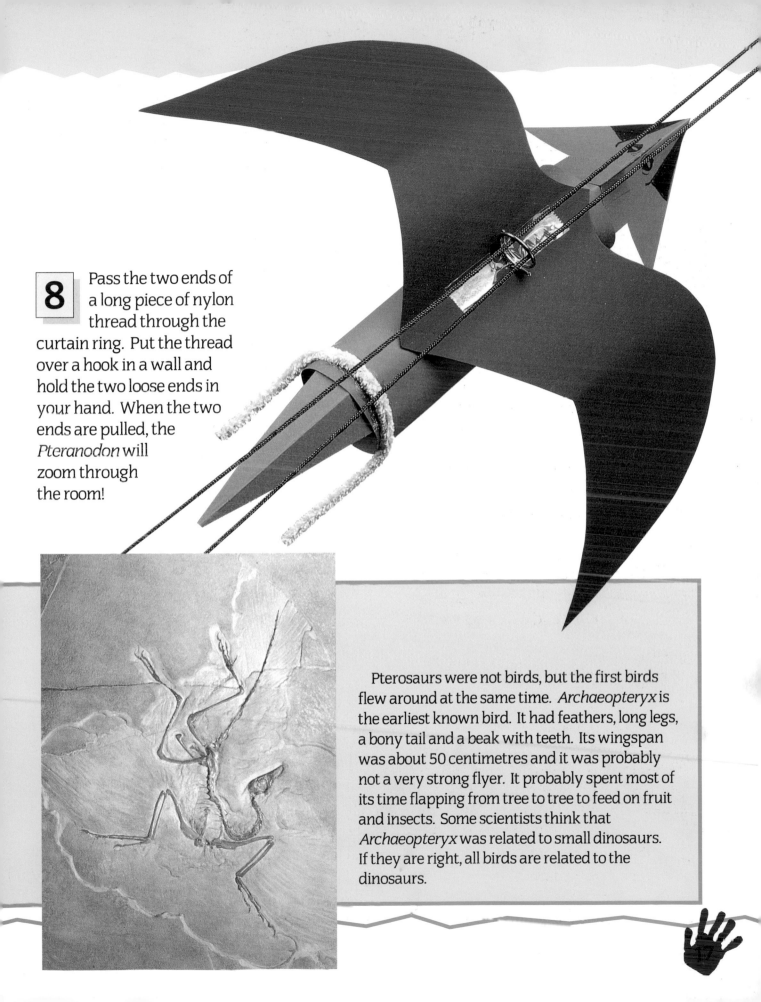

8 Pass the two ends of a long piece of nylon thread through the curtain ring. Put the thread over a hook in a wall and hold the two loose ends in your hand. When the two ends are pulled, the *Pteranodon* will zoom through the room!

Pterosaurs were not birds, but the first birds flew around at the same time. *Archaeopteryx* is the earliest known bird. It had feathers, long legs, a bony tail and a beak with teeth. Its wingspan was about 50 centimetres and it was probably not a very strong flyer. It probably spent most of its time flapping from tree to tree to feed on fruit and insects. Some scientists think that *Archaeopteryx* was related to small dinosaurs. If they are right, all birds are related to the dinosaurs.

Giant Tooth

YOU WILL NEED:
- air-hardening clay
- well-marked stones
- water-colour inks
- tan boot polish
- cloth

MESSY ACTIVITY

1 To copy a dinosaur tooth, model a big ball of clay into a shape similar to that shown here. Keep your hands wet while you are working.

Dinosaur Teeth

Teeth make good fossils because they are hard and do not quickly disappear through decay. One of the first dinosaur fossils to be found was a jaw bone with a tooth still in it. In 1824, William Buckland named the animal *Megalosaurus* ("big lizard"). Meat-eaters like *Megalosaurus* had sharp teeth, often with edges like those of a saw. A large biting tooth from the great meat-eater *Allosaurus* (right) was found to be 17 centimetres long.

Plant-eaters had smaller, blunter teeth to chop and grind up their food. Some also had a beak at the front of their mouth to help them gather up and eat big mouthfuls of plants. *Iguanodon*, for example, had a narrow skull and a pointed beak.

Plant-eaters deliberately swallowed "gizzard stones", called gastroliths. These stones in the stomach helped to crush the leaves, making them easier to digest.

A duck-billed dinosaur could have as many as 700 teeth!

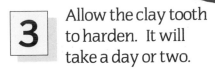

2 Texture the surface of the clay by pressing it against a stone or rock. Peel off the clay and mark it with stone patterns all around to give it a fossilized look.

3 Allow the clay tooth to harden. It will take a day or two.

4 Now paint the tooth., using brown and ochre inks. You can apply the paint in any way that you like.

5 When the paint is dry, rub tan boot polish into the clay to make it look shiny and weathered. The tooth makes a good paperweight.

Home-made Apatosaurus

MESSY ACTIVITY

1 Assemble the body of your *Apatosaurus* first. Cut two toilet rolls in half to make the legs. Tape the legs to the bottle with parcel tape.

YOU WILL NEED:
✓large plastic bottle ✓kitchen paper tube ✓4 toilet roll tubes
✓pencil ✓ruler ✓thin card ✓coloured tissue paper ✓scissors
✓parcel tape ✓2 buttons ✓fungicide-free wallpaper paste
✓varnish ✓glue brush ✓newspaper

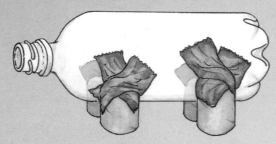

2 Make the long neck and the small head by cutting a toilet roll in half and cutting a segment out of each side. Tape the toilet roll to a kitchen paper tube and attach it to the top of the bottle with more parcel tape.

3 For the tail, draw around a saucer onto some card and cut out the circle. Cut out a section from the circle, roll it into a cone and fasten the edges. Stick the cone into the remaining half-toilet roll and then tape the tail to the bottom of the bottle.

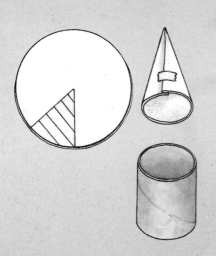

4 Tear some newspaper into thin strips (about 5 cm wide). Mix up the paste as instructed on the packet, and coat each strip of paper with it. Cover the model with at least four layers of paste-coated paper.

Plant-eaters

Apatosaurus ("headless lizard") was an enormous long-necked plant-eater. It was over 20 metres long and weighed about 30 tonnes. It used its long neck to reach the tree tops, where it gathered leaves to eat.

It had a very small head, which accounts for its name. It had long, delicate teeth, which may mean that it spent a lot of time in lakes and rivers, feeding on tender water plants. Its tail was very long and was whip-like at the end.

Scientists used to call it *Brontosaurus* until they realised that *Brontosaurus* fossils were the same as *Apatosaurus*. Since one dinosaur cannot have two different names, *Apatosaurus* was chosen.

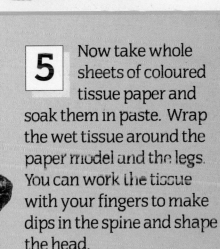

5 Now take whole sheets of coloured tissue paper and soak them in paste. Wrap the wet tissue around the paper model and the legs. You can work the tissue with your fingers to make dips in the spine and shape the head.

6 When your *Apatosaurus* is dry, stick on two button eyes and varnish the whole model.

Imagine what the real *Apatosaurus* was like at over 20 metres long!

Nest Eggs

YOU WILL NEED:
- ✔ newspaper ✔ PVA glue ✔ poster paint
- ✔ leaves ✔ air-hardening clay ✔ ruler
- ✔ brown and yellow tissue paper ✔ water
- ✔ large round ice-cream or margarine tub

1 To make big dinosaur eggs, screw a whole double sheet of newspaper into a ball. Screw it up very tightly.

2 Make several pats of clay and cover the paper ball with them. Moisten the joints and smear them together.

3 Beat the ball into an egg shape with a ruler. This will make the egg smooth and strong.

Nest eggs

We know from fossils that dinosaurs laid shelled eggs on land. Fossilized eggs and young *Protoceratops* have been found in the Gobi desert in Mongolia. The eggs were over 15 centimetres long. These large eggs were protected from drying out by their tough, waterproof shell. Safe inside the shell, the young dinosaur was nourished by a large supply of yolk, until it was ready to hatch out.

It is believed that dinosaurs often laid their eggs in the sand or in mud nests on high ground, away from water.

4 Make some smaller eggs in the same way, and let them dry.

5 You can paint the eggs different colours with patterns of your own choice as we don't know what markings dinosaur eggs had.

6 The eggs need a nest. Screw small pieces of tissue paper into balls. Stick them all over the outside of a large round tub.

7 Make a cushion of tissue paper in your nest and put the eggs in. Cover them up with leaves just in case an egg-eating dinosaur, such as an *Oviraptor*, is on the look-out for a snack.

Oviraptor means "egg-thief".

Catch a Diplodocus

1 For this game, cut one side off a cereal box to make a tray. Tape the open end to close it up. Strengthen all the corners with sticky tape.

YOU WILL NEED:
✔ *empty cereal box* ✔ *straws* ✔ *scissors* ✔ *felt pens* ✔ *glue stick*
✔ *large plastic washing up liquid bottle* ✔ *white cartridge paper*
✔ *stapler* ✔ *sticky tape* ✔ *corrugated paper*

2 Cut a strip of corrugated paper to fit the sides of the tray- with the lines running vertically. Staple or glue the corrugated paper strip around the outside rim of the tray. Add some vegetation inside the tray.

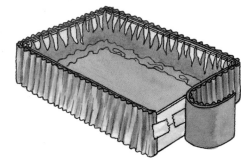

3 Copy or trace this *Diplodocus*. Make sure it has a long neck to fit around a straw. Draw, colour and cut out five *Diplodocus* heads.

4 Write a number on each head and tape it onto a straw. Stick the straws into the corrugated sides of the tray.

5 Ask and adult to help you carefully cut 1 cm wide rings from a washing-up liquid bottle and colour them.

6 To play the game, throw the rings and see how many *Diplodocuses* you can catch. Add up the score after each round.

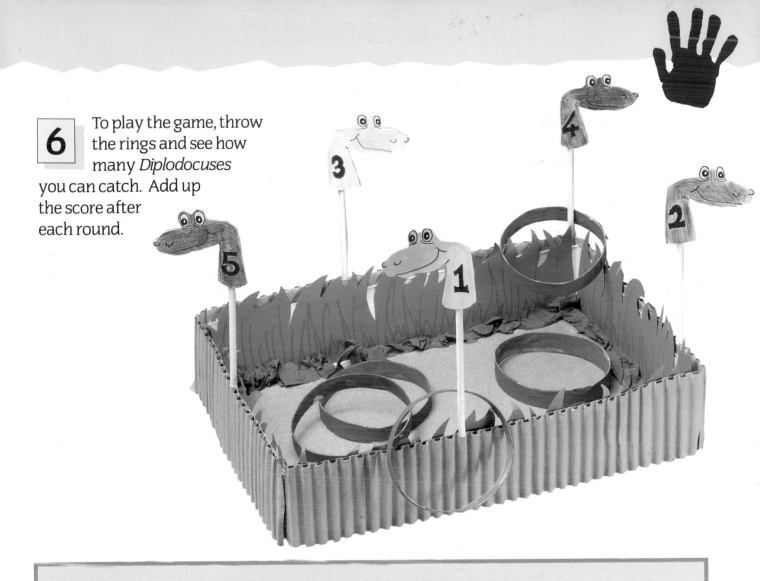

Diplodocus

Diplodocus (below left) was one of the longest land animals ever known. It was about 27 metres long - about as long as eight cars parked end to end! Most of its length was made up by its thin neck and tail. It weighed about 10 tonnes and so was not one of the heaviest dinosaurs.

Its name means "double beam". This comes from the two bony skids that protected its tail as it was dragged along the ground.

Diplodocus was a plant-eater, and scientists used to think that it lived in lakes and swamps. But this is now believed to be unlikely, because it had small feet compared with its body. It would have found it difficult to walk on swampy ground without sinking in. Today it is thought that *Diplodocus* lived on land, using its long neck to reach leaves in the tops of tall trees.

Pop-up Pliosaurus

YOU WILL NEED
- ✔ thick white card 30 cm x 25cm
- ✔ thin card ✔ masking tape
- ✔ felt pens ✔ ruler ✔ pencil
- ✔ sticky tape ✔ scissors
- ✔ tracing paper

1 Fold the card in half.

2 With tracing paper and a pencil, trace the *Pliosaurus* mouth, sharp teeth and tabs and cut out the shape.

Sea Reptiles

None of the dinosaurs actually lived in the sea. But many large sea reptiles did exist in the age of dinosaurs. *Plesiosaurs* looked rather like dinosaurs. They had long necks, but their bodies were round and had paddle-like flippers. They probably fed on fish, which they snapped up with their sharp pointed teeth.

Pliosaurs were short-necked plesiosaurs and were very big - the whales of the prehistoric seas.

Ichthyosaurs ("fish lizards") were up to 12 metres long and looked similar to the dolphins of today. Like dolphins, they came to the surface to breathe, and they also gave birth to live young in the water. Lurking in rivers and coastal waters were early crocodiles, ready to snap at any unwary animals that came within range of their large jaws.

3 Fold a piece of thin card - it must be big enough for the length and width of the tracing to fit on. Now place the tracing paper mouth along the fold and draw round it. This will be one jaw.

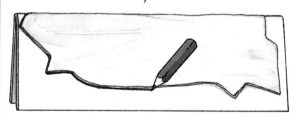

4 Make the other jaw in the same way on another piece of thin card. You now have two identical jaws.

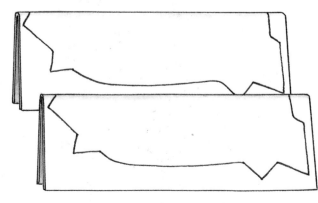

5 Cut out the jaws - but don't cut the fold - and open them out. Then colour them in - green outside and red inside.

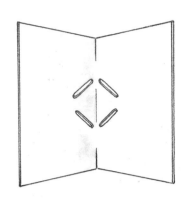

6 Ask an adult to cut four slits into the piece of thick card as shown here. The cuts start 1/2 cm from the centre fold of the card. The gap between the jaws should be no larger than 5 cm to allow the jaws to close properly.

7 Before putting the tabs through the slits, fold each jaw in half. Then open it up a little and push the tabs through the slits. Open and close the card to check that it works. You might have to adjust the tabs slightly before securing them with tape on the front and back of the card.

8 Now draw eyes, fins and a tail on the card to complete your pop-up *Pliosaurus*.

9 Draw a sea picture on the outside of the card and send it to a friend.

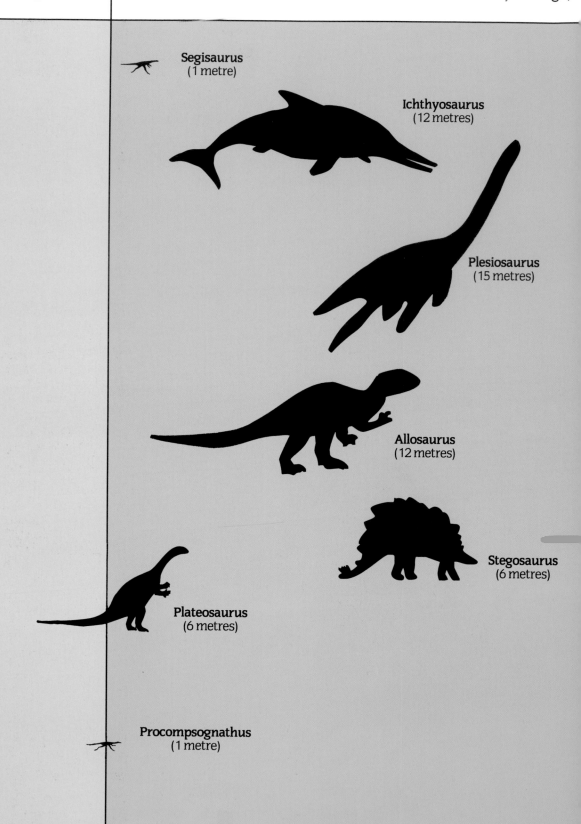

Segisaurus
(1 metre)

Ichthyosaurus
(12 metres)

Plesiosaurus
(15 metres)

Allosaurus
(12 metres)

Stegosaurus
(6 metres)

Plateosaurus
(6 metres)

Procompsognathus
(1 metre)

Iguanodon
(10 metres)

Pteranodon
(7 metres)

Protoceratops
(1.8 metres)

Torosaurus
(7 metres)

Diplodocus
(27 metres)

Tyrannosaurus
(14 metres)

Apatosaurus
(21 metres)

The end of the dinosaurs

All dinosaurs died out about 65 million years ago. It is not known definitely why this happened, but there are a lot of theories. It is thought that a huge meteorite crashed into the Earth and sent up a thick cloud of dust. This may have blocked out the sun's warmth, and the dinosaurs may have frozen to death.

29

Glossary

amphibian - an animal that can live both on land and in water, such as a frog.

continent - one of the earth's large land masses.

Cretaceous period - the third and last part of the Mesozoic era, from 144 to 65 million years ago. Dinosaurs died out at the end of this period.

dinosaur - an extinct form of reptile that lived on Earth for 165 million years.

fossil - the remains of animals or plants preserved in rocks. They include bones, teeth and footprints.

hatch - to emerge from an egg.

ichthyosaur - a sea reptile related to the dinosaurs. It was similar to the dolphin of today.

iguana - a large South American lizard.

Jurassic period - the second part of the Mesozoic era, from 213 to 144 million years ago, when dinosaurs flourished.

mammal - a warm-blooded backboned animal whose young feed on their mother's milk.

Mesozoic era - "Middle life" - the third of the four main lengths of time which we use to divide up the Earth's history. It lasted from 240 to 65 million years ago and is divided into three periods - the Triassic, Jurassic and Cretaceous.

meteorite - a lump of rock or metal that falls to Earth from outer space.

plesiosaur - a sea reptile related to the dinosaurs that swam with flippers.

pliosaur - a very big, short-necked plesiosaur.

prey - an animal hunted by another for food.

pterosaur - a winged reptile related to the dinosaurs.

reptile - a cold-blooded backboned animal, such as snakes, lizards and crocodiles. Dinosaurs were reptiles.

skeleton - the hard framework of bones that supports and protects the soft parts of an animal's body.

skull - the bony skeleton of the head.

swamp - ground that is always wet and usually overgrown with plants and trees.

theory - an idea about something, such as a scientist's idea about what happened and why.

Triassic period - the first part of the Mesozoic era, from 248 to 213 million years ago, when dinosaurs first appeared.

yolk - the part of an egg that nourishes the developing young animal.

Useful Websites

www.bbc.co.uk/dinosaurs
includes factfiles on all your favourite dinosaurs, and the unusual ones too. It includes a timeline and dinosaur games, such as designing your very own dinosaur!

www.enchantedlearning.com/ subjects/dinosaurs includes factfiles, tips for identifying dinosaurs and fun things to do, such as dinosaur printouts for colouring-in and dinosaur quizzes.

www.kidsdomain.com/craft provides step-by-step illustrated instructions for a range of themed craft activities including making things from from recycled objects.

www.crafts4kids.com includes a variety of craft projects including how to make Dinosaur Soap. Step-by-step instructions are given, as well as printable templates.

Places to visit
United Kingdom
The Natural History Museum
Cromwell Road, London SW7 5BD
www.nhm.ac.uk

The Dinosaur Museum
Icen Way, Dorchester, Dorset
www.dinosaur-museum.org.uk

Dinosaurland
Coombe Street, Lyme Regis
Dorset DT7 3PY
www.dinosaurland.co.uk

Australia
National Dinosaur Museum
Gold Creek Village, Gungahlin
Canberra ACT 2912
www.nationaldinosaurmuseum.com.au

The Queensland Museum
Grey and Melbourne Streets
South Bank, South Brisbane
www.qmuseum.qld.gov.au

Note to parents and teachers
Every effort has been made by the Publishers to ensure that these websites are suitable for children; that they are of the highest educational value, and that they contain no inappropriate or offensive material. However, because of the nature of the Internet, it is impossible to guarantee that the contents of these sites will not be altered. We strongly advise that Internet access is supervised by a responsible adult.

Index

Additional photographs:
The Natural History Museum, London 15(tr),
25(b); Pat Morris 11(l), 17(b), 18(l), 22(bl).

KT-497-745

Would you like to join an exciting expedition to Egypt?

The characters accompanying you on the expedition, Will Yates, Dr. Jane Smith and Dr. Mokhtar Ahmad, are fictional. But real facts about Egyptologists, archaeologists and scientists have been used to give you an accurate picture of the work they do. The tomb you will help to discover and the mummy buried inside are also fictional. But the characteristics of the mummy and details from the excavation are based on real-life discoveries made in Egypt. .

Interested to know more? Ready to dig for ancient clues?
Then welcome to the City Museum...

CONTENTS

CITY MUSEUM PASS

Name: Dr. Jane Smith
Department: Head of Ancient Egyptian Antiquities

Interests: Ancient civilizations, travel and digging.

TEMPORARY

CITY MUSEUM PASS

Name: Will Yates
Department: Ancient Egyptian Antiquities – temporary research assistant

Interests: Ancient history, computers and old horror movies!

TREASURES IN THE ATTIC

Day 1

Today has been so exciting! We visited Dr. Smith, a curator at the City Museum, to show her the things we'd found in the attic. There's a very old diary and postcards, a tiny statue, a golden beetle and some tools. Dad thinks that my Great Grandpa must have brought them back from his travels to Egypt.

Dr. Smith showed me around behind the scenes at the museum. There's a library packed with old books and the latest computers, miles of storage shelves piled high with labelled boxes and a big science laboratory. This is where they 'conserve' (that's the museum word for investigate and look after) the objects in their collections.

Dr. Smith is an Egyptologist, an expert on ancient Egypt. She looked at everything we'd brought in and read some of the diary. She thinks that Great Grandpa may have found an important site. Possibly even an ancient Egyptian tomb!

1st November 1935
Mrs. Henrietta Yates

My dear Henrietta,

Arrived safely yesterday. It is very hot and dusty. Tomorrow we are going by camel to see some interesting ruins. Camels are perfectly designed for desert travel. They store gallons of water in their bodies and have broad feet for walking on sand. I hope I don't fall off!

Your loving husband
Bertie

Small clay statue. Dr. Smith says it looks like a 'shabti' figure. They were placed in tombs in ancient Egypt.

Egypt, on the continent of Africa, where Great Grandpa went exploring!

Dr. Smith says the digging season in Egypt was in the winter, when it was cooler.

This golden beetle is called a 'scarab'. They were ancient Egyptian good-luck charms.

my old friend Ibrahim. He helped me explore my first ancient Egyptian site.

18th November 1935

Another hard day spent digging. Found some strange artefacts and a huge piece of stone covered in carvings. Am not yet sure what they are, or why they are here. Have to go home next week, but will sketch the place where I made the discoveries, and will try to find the site again when I return next year.

From: Dr. Jane Smith, The City Museum
To: Dr. Mokhtar Ahmad, Cairo, Egypt
Subject: An exciting new discovery!
Dear Mokhtar,
An interesting old diary and a collection of ancient Egyptian objects have been brought to our Museum. I think they could be clues to an important site. Our problem is how to find it. The diary contains only a rough sketch of the place and a scribbled place-name.
Please can you help us?
From: Dr. Mokhtar Ahmad, Cairo, Egypt
To: Dr. Jane Smith, The City Museum
Dear Jane,
We have looked up the place-name on local maps, but I'm afraid we cannot find it. Perhaps the man who wrote the diary did not understand Arabic, our language, and made a mistake. We will try to find out more. Maybe we could try exploring the region, and compare the old sketch with the landscape.

A TRIP TO EGYPT

Day 21

We are on a plane flying over Egypt!
I couldn't believe it when Dr. Smith told me
that her old friend Dr. Ahmad wanted to
mount an expedition to find out more about
the place Great Grandpa discovered. I was
even more surprised when she said I could
come along as her research assistant.

It won't be long now before we land. From
the window I can see the famous pyramids,
the desert and the River Nile, all far below.
At first we'll stay in Cairo, that's the
modern capital city of Egypt. It's strange to
think that it didn't exist in ancient Egyptian
times. The Nile flows right through Cairo, and
there are now buildings on both banks of the
river. In ancient Egyptian times cities were
built on the east, or right-hand, bank only.

I've sketched out a map of Egypt showing
all the most important ancient and modern
sites, while enjoying some delicious mezze.
This traditional Egyptian snack includes bread,
hoummous, olives and stuffed grape leaves.

The River Nile flowing through
the bustling modern city of Cairo.

The Sahara is the world's largest desert. It stretches across the north of Africa dominating the landscape of many African countries, including Egypt.

Map of Egypt along the banks of the River Nile

Mediterranean Sea

Great Pyramids, Giza

Saqqara (city of the dead)

Lower Egypt

Cairo

Memphis (ancient capital of Lower Egypt)

Lake Karun

Fertile land

Upper Egypt

River Nile flows north

West bank of the Nile: 'the land of the dead'.

East bank of the Nile: 'the land of the living'.

Red Sea

Valley of the Kings

Desert oasis

Desert

Thebes (the ancient capital of Upper Egypt) and Karnak (a massive temple complex)

Aswan High Dam (collects Nile floodwater)

Abu Simbel (temples and huge statues)

From: Dr. Mokhtar Ahmad, Cairo, Egypt
To: Dr. Jane Smith, The City Museum
Subject: Good news – come quickly!

Dear Jane,

We think we've found the site mentioned in the old diary. It's in a remote part of Egypt on the west, or left-hand, bank of the Nile. The ancient Egyptians associated dying with the setting of the sun. The sun sets in the west so they buried their dead on the west bank. We found the place completely by chance! One of my colleagues recognised the land formation from a picture in a newspaper article about a new hotel that is planned in the area. We have contacted the developers, and they are due to start work soon. We are planning to explore the site as quickly as possible. Would you like to join us? It would be wonderful to see you again.

EARLY EGYPTIAN EXPLORERS

Day 22

I've just spent a fascinating afternoon with Dr. Ahmad, finding out as much as I can about Egypt and ancient Egyptian tombs. I wanted to know more about archaeologists too. They are scientists who study human life in the past by excavating and investigating everyday items. Dr. Ahmad unearthed an old illustration and some battered black and white photographs of early archaeologists at work in Egypt. Then he showed me a plan of one of the most famous tombs ever discovered: Tutankhamun's tomb.

Tutankhamun became pharaoh (that was what the ancient Egyptians called their kings) when he was nine years old, in 1336 BC. When he died, aged just 18, he was buried in an underground tomb in a place called the Valley of the Kings. An archaeologist called Howard Carter discovered the tomb in 1922. Dr. Smith says that no other single excavation has given us so much evidence about life in ancient Egypt.

Carter at work in Tutankhamun's tomb. He was the first person to see inside the tomb for over 3,250 years.

Tutankhamun's Tomb

This room contained three coffins, one inside the other! In the final solid gold coffin was Tutankhamun's mummified (preserved) body.

THE BURIAL CHAMBER

THE ANNEXE
(extra storage space)

THE ANTECHAMBE

THE DISCOVERY
When Carter and his team excavated Tutankhamun's tomb they found it contained four rooms. It took ten years to carefully empty the tomb of all its treasures!

1923: Howard Carter inspects the site.

Abu Simbel, the Great Temple, in 1817. Before photography was invented artists painted pictures to record discoveries.

This room contained over 500 beautiful objects – jewellery, statues and model boats.

THE TREASURY

Abu Simbel is now fully excavated. In the 1960s it was even moved from its original site when a huge lake was created by the building of the Aswan High Dam. The temple would have been covered by water so it was moved piece by piece to a safe place beside the lake.

Carter's team had to tunnel through a rubble filled corridor and break through two sealed doors to get to the tomb.

The buried, secret entrance to the tomb.

STAIRWELL

CORRIDOR

This room was packed with useful items Tutankhamun would need in the next world, including food, clothes, jewellery, furniture, weapons and even chariots.

The Antechamber as Carter first saw it.

From: Will Yates
To: City School History Club
Subject: Ancient Egyptian tombs

Hi Guys,

We are all very excited about the possibility of there being an undiscovered tomb buried somewhere in Egypt. Apparently the ancient Egyptians built all sorts of elaborate tombs. They believed that when a person died their spirit travelled into the 'Next World' – a beautiful place filled with sunshine and happiness, where life was everlasting. They preserved the bodies of the dead (I'm going to find out more about this) and filled their tombs with useful items that they might need in the 'Next World'. Little statues like Great Grandpa's shabti figure were put into tombs as well. They were there to do the work of the dead person. Wealthy Egyptians sometimes had 365 shabtis in their tombs, one to do the work for each day of the year! I'm doing some more research, and will be in touch again soon.

USER 1
USER 2
USER 3

Day 23

This morning we headed straight for the Egyptian Museum, here in Cairo. During the 19th century Egypt became a magnet for treasure hunters, and many precious objects were collected to be sold. Items that were not saleable were just thrown away! In 1835 the Egyptian government set up the museum so that ancient treasures from the archaeological sites could be collected in one place and protected. First we visited the special Tutankhamun galleries. They contain over 1700 items, all from his tomb. I particularly wanted to see Tutankhamun's famous gold death mask. This magnificent mask was made from two layers of gold that were hammered together and inlaid with semiprecious stones. It weighs just over 10 kg and is 54 cm high.

I was keen to find out some more about shabtis as well. It seems they could be carved out of wood or stone, moulded from clay or glass, cast from bronze or wax or shaped by hand from faience: a glazed ceramic material.

TUTANKHAMUN'S DEATH MASK
This gold death mask shows a portrait of Tutankhamun. Death masks were placed on the faces of mummies to help the spirits recognise their bodies.

Ancient Egyptian Crafts - Making a Shabti

Step 1. First make the faience by adding a little lime and ash to crushed quartz. Then mix it with water to make a paste.

Step 2. Shape it by hand to look like a mummy.

Step 3. Leave it to dry.

Step 4. Rub the surface with a pebble to give a smooth, shiny finish (this is called burnishing).

Step 5. Paint on extra details, if required.

Step 6. Arrange on a metal grid at the bottom of a brick kiln.

Step 7. Light a fire underneath to fire (bake) the clay.

TOMB PAINTINGS

Tombs were decorated with painted scenes showing the dead person's journey to the 'Next World'. They faced many tests and dangers. In one test their heart was weighed to judge their past behaviour. If it was too heavy – they had been bad – it was eaten by a crocodile-headed goddess called Ammut. Their spirit would die, and they would never reach the 'Next World'.

Here we see Tutankhamun welcomed into the realms of the dead by the ancient Egyptian goddess Nut.

ANUBIS

The ancient Egyptians had many gods. This statue portrays Anubis, the jackal-headed god of the dead.

FIT FOR A KING

This magnificent coffin is made of gold-covered wood, studded with crimson glass and blue pottery. It is the second (middle) of the three glittering coffins made to house the mummified remains of Tutankhamun's body.

AT THE PYRAMIDS

Day 24

Today we visited the pyramids at Giza, on the west bank of the river. They are awesome! No wonder people call them one of the 'Seven Wonders of the World'. Dr. Smith says the Great Pyramid is 147 metres high and weighs 6 million tonnes. Ever since it was finished, about 4,500 years ago, it's been the biggest stone building in the world. It took 100,000 men about 20 years to build. They had to cut and shape 2.3 million blocks of stone; then move them using just ropes and wooden rollers. The ancient Egyptian builders had no machinery to help them, and no-one knows for sure how they lifted the blocks up to the top.

Our Egyptian guide told me that the pyramids were built as burial chambers for pharaohs. It was believed that their sloping shape helped the pharaoh's spirit climb up to the sky. He also taught me an old Arab saying. 'People fear time, but time fears the pyramids!'

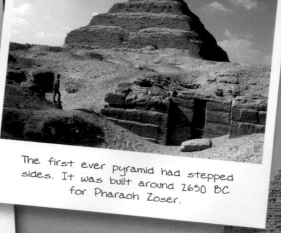

The first ever pyramid had stepped sides. It was built around 2650 BC for Pharaoh Zoser.

Here I am painting the Sphinx. This kindly stone monster has guarded the pyramids for 4,500 years.

Dear Mum

Egypt is brilliant. This ancient carving shows pyramid-builders working with very simple tools. The stonemasons' work had to be extremely precise or else the pyramid blocks wouldn't have slotted together. Will write again soon.

The three pyramids at Giza were originally covered with white limestone and capped with gold. Today, only a bit of the covering remains - and it's no longer white! The gold was stolen long ago.

The sphinx has a lion's body and a man's head. It used to have a false beard, but this has worn away over the centuries. Pharaohs often wore a false beard as a symbol of their kingship.

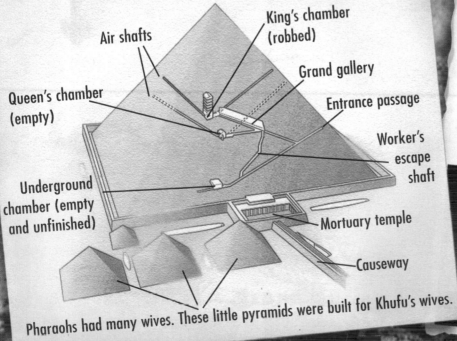

The Great Pyramid was built around 2551 BC by Pharaoh Khufu. He was buried in the King's chamber.

Air shafts

King's chamber (robbed)

Grand gallery

Queen's chamber (empty)

Entrance passage

Worker's escape shaft

Underground chamber (empty and unfinished)

Mortuary temple

Causeway

Pharaohs had many wives. These little pyramids were built for Khufu's wives.

PYRAMIDS BUILT BY SPACE INVADERS?

Egyptologists will be amused to hear of the many wild ideas to be discussed today at a conference of pyramid enthusiasts from around the world. According to one speaker, creatures from outer space will one day re-visit the pyramids and bring the dead pharaohs back to life. Rival speakers will suggest that the pyramids were temples used for human sacrifices, monuments built by Bible-story hero Noah after he survived the Great Flood or giant storage silos for grain. The conference will also consider claims that the shape of the pyramids has the power to turn dead bodies into mummies, focus healing energy and sharpen razor blades!

THE RIVER NILE

Day 25

We are on our way to Great Grandpa's site, travelling south from Cairo in a four-wheel drive landcruiser. A camel ride would have been much more exciting! We're heading for the desert, but so far we've stayed close to the River Nile. That's where most people live, just like in ancient Egyptian times. Almost every year, from June to September, the Nile flooded the land on either side of its banks. But since the 1960s the floods have been controlled by the massive Aswan Dam. Apart from a few desert oases (water holes where plants and trees grow) the Nile is the only source of water in Egypt. It was important to the ancient Egyptians for another reason too. Sailing up and down the river was by far the quickest way to travel in those days.

Dr. Smith says the climate in Egypt hasn't changed much over the centuries; it hardly ever rains, is very hot in daytime and very cold at night.

The pyramid complex at Giza in Great Grandpa's day. This is during the annual flood before the Aswan High Dam was built.

The Nile is the longest river in the world. It flows north for 6671 km, from Lake Victoria in East Africa to the Mediterranean Sea.

In ancient Egypt there wasn't much wood around. Most boats were made from bundles of papyrus, a tough reed that grew on the banks of the river.

This is a side view of a huge stone staircase called a Nilometer. The stairs lead down into the River Nile. During the annual flood the ancient Egyptians watched to see how high up the stairs the water rose. If it was too low there wouldn't be enough water to grow food. But if it rose too high the fields would be washed away. Records were kept of the river's rise and fall.

In ancient Egypt the Nile bustled with passenger ferries, fishing boats and barges carrying cattle, grain and slabs of stone for building projects. Today, Nile sailing boats called feluccas still carry many Egyptian goods and passengers.

From: Will Yates
To: City School History Club
Subject: On the banks of the River Nile

Hi Guys,

I've seen a real scorpion! They live under rocks and in cracks in the ground. Dr. Smith says I should look inside my trainers every morning before I put them on. There are mosquitos buzzing everywhere too. I've covered my face and hands in insect repellant, as mosquito-bites carry malaria and other dangerous diseases.

Today Dr. Smith took me to the banks of the River Nile to look at some of the black river mud. It was so stinky, but Dr. Smith says the ancient Egyptians called it 'the gift of the Nile'. After the annual floods the farmers could grow their food in the mud: crops like wheat and barley, fruit like grapes, dates and melons and vegetables like beans, leeks, cucumbers and onions. How gross! But without this fertile land between the river and the desert Dr. Smith says the ancient Egyptians would have starved.

USER 1

USER 2

USER 3

AT THE DIG SITE

Day 26

I'm exhausted! But at long last we've arrived. It's not easy driving across the desert. There are no roads, and the ground is very bumpy. We finally found the site by comparing the sketch in Great Grandpa's diary with some rocks we could see far away on the horizon. As we got closer we could also see the Egyptian archaeologists and teams of Egyptian labourers.

The archaeologists had dug a trial trench across one side of the site, and had mapped out the area using pegs with string stretched across to make a large grid. The lead archaeologist had then drawn a grid-sheet (a kind of map) that corresponded to the grid on the ground. The map is then used to record the position of all the 'finds' (objects uncovered on the site) before they are moved. We could hardly wait to discover what they had found. But we got a shock when we asked them. 'Nothing yet' they said. 'We're beginning to wonder whether this is the right place after all.'

Working slowly and carefully, archaeologists use soft brushes and trowels to remove layers of soil from the site.

We found the site using Great Grandpa's sketch in his diary.

GRID SHEET

Key to map of site

1. Outcrop of rocky hills
2. Large rocks
3. Main trench
4. Palm tree stumps
5. Mud bricks
6. A Roman coin
7. Stony areas

Archaeologists wear masks to avoid breathing in dust, and hard hats to protect their heads from falling stones and collapsing trenches.

Finds are stored in bags or boxes labelled with the name of the site and where the item was found.

Long tape-measures and stripy poles, marked in metres and centimetres, are used to measure the site and record the position of finds.

Sand and soil are gently shaken through a fine metal screen to collect tiny fragments of evidence, such as teeth or seeds.

Day 30

Yesterday was terrible! We'd still found absolutely nothing. Then at lunchtime a huge digger arrived and parked a little way from our site. It was followed by a surveyor and an engineer. They told us work was now due to start on the new hotel.

We dug desperately for the rest of the day, but finding nothing went to bed very gloomy. Then first thing this morning something amazing happened. As the digger-driver started up his machine, the digger's back wheels began to sink into the sand and gravel. As the driver tried to clear away the sand, he discovered a chunk of rock covered in elaborate carvings. Dr. Smith immediately recognised the carvings as hieroglyphs, the picture writing used by the ancient Egyptians. As we brushed away the sand, Dr. Smith explained that there were around 1000 different picture symbols. Each one represented a sound or a person, an object or an idea. Temples and tombs were covered in hieroglyphs. Could we have discovered the entrance to an underground tomb?

Close to the entrance of important tombs was a mortuary (funeral) temple. The temples were decorated with tall pillars.

The ground collapses under the weight of the heavy digger.

Pottery bowls of bread, meat (usually roasted ducks), beer, water or wine were left in tombs as offerings, to feed the spirit of the dead person.

Important tombs were marked with stele – slabs of wood or stone. They were decorated with paintings or carvings of the dead person and hieroglyphs of their name.

The 'Rosetta Stone' at the British Museum in London.

From: Dr. Mokhtar Ahmad, Cairo, Egypt
To: Will Yates
Subject: Ancient Egyptian Hieroglyphs

Dear Will,

The carvings you describe are indeed hieroglyphs. They were invented around 3100 BC, and were used mostly for religious or royal texts. Very few people could read or write in ancient Egypt. Those who could were called scribes. They held all the most important jobs, working in the temples or keeping records for the pharaoh. Early archaeologists couldn't read the carvings, but in 1822 a French scholar Jean-François Champollion cracked the ancient hieroglyph code using the Rosetta Stone. This huge stone was carved with the same words in three different types of writing – hieroglyphs, Egyptian demotic writing (a later form of writing that turned hieroglyphs into shapes like letters) and ancient Greek. Champollion used his knowledge of ancient Greek to work out how to read the other two!

USER 1

USER 2

USER 3

Day 35

I'm hot, exhausted and I ache all over! The developers have agreed to postpone their work so there's no time to waste. Dr. Smith has let me help with the digging, but I have to be very careful as inexperienced diggers can accidentally damage important artefacts. I've spent days on my hands and knees gently sweeping away layers of sand with a brush. But all the hard work has been worthwhile. We've uncovered an underground passageway and some fabulous real Egyptian treasures!

Ancient Egyptian tomb robbers were here before us though. We found evidence of the equipment they used to break into the tomb. They had stone hammers with wooden handles, saws and chisels with copper blades and reed baskets, for carrying their loot. Luckily they must have been disturbed as we've found many items buried in the sand outside the tomb, including a pair of gold earrings. As only the rich could afford real gold jewellery, Dr. Smith thinks the tomb was made for a rich woman; maybe even an Egyptian princess.

DESIGNERS IN THE DESERT

We know a great deal about ancient Egyptian fashion from paintings and statues. Wealthy women wore long dresses of fine white linen, crinkled into hundreds of clinging pleats. Over the top they wore wide jewelled collars and sometimes see-through tunics of netting, decorated with glass beads. Sandals made of plaited papyrus reeds completed the look.

Glass was made from sand and natron (a salty chemical). This glass bottle was probably used for scent or skin-softening oil.

A little dish with a handle shaped like a slave girl. It contains traces of coloured powder. Probably used for cosmetics.

Fragments of smashed faience. Are they the remains of shabti figures dropped by the tomb robbers as they ran away?

A damaged section from a jewelled collar. These were worn over dresses and tunics. The blue stones are lapis lazuli.

From: Will Yates
To: Kate Yates, City College
Subject: Ancient Egyptian beauty tips

Hi Sis,

The dig is going really well, and you are going to love what we found today – some make-up that is over 3,500 years old! Dr. Smith warned me not to touch it as it might be full of ancient germs. Apparently both men and women wore make-up in ancient Egypt. They used crushed black or green stone mixed with water for eyeliner, and they mixed powdered red ochre (earth) with animal fat to colour their cheeks and lips. They wore perfume too. I know because we've found an actual perfume bottle! And although I knew ancient Egyptian women liked to wear long curly or plaited wigs made from human hair – I didn't know they shaved their heads underneath!

Tweezers pick up objects that are too small or too delicate to be moved by hand.

USER 1
USER 2
USER 3

INSIDE THE TOMB

Day 42

I now know how it feels to make an amazing discovery, just like Howard Carter! The passage into the tomb was almost blocked where the roof had fallen in, and was too dangerous for a person to squeeze through. The team decided to use an experimental, new type of remote control robot. The robot's camera sent back pictures to a special computer screen. At first all we could see was darkness. But then flickering images of carvings and wall-paintings appeared on the screen. The robot moved very slowly. But as it turned its lights towards the centre of the burial chamber, we found ourselves face to face with a beautiful mummy!

Dr. Smith explained that the ancient Egyptians preserved their bodies in order to fully enjoy the Next World. Egypt's hot, dry atmosphere naturally dried out corpses, but when the process of mummification was developed it meant that dead bodies could be preserved for all time.

Archaeology Today - Special Report
ROBOT ARCHAEOLOGISTS

Testing a robot designed to explore a small shaft inside the Great Pyramid.

An extraordinary engineering feat, this robot is compact enough to navigate narrow places, but can carry a huge amount of scientific equipment. Could this new technology be the way forward? Places that are too small or dangerous for a human archaeologist could be navigated by remote-controlled robots fitted with fibre-optic cameras.

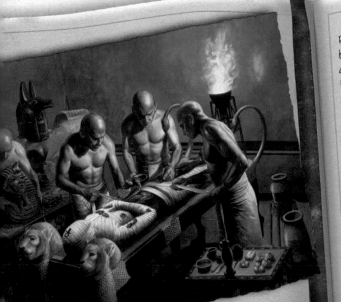

How to make a mummy

First push a metal hook up the nose, and pull the brain out. Then make a cut in the body's left side, and pull out the heart, lungs, liver, stomach and intestines. Rinse the empty body with wine and spices, and pack full of natron. Cover the body with natron, and leave for up to 70 days. The natron will absorb the water from the flesh. Put the heart back in the body. Wrap the dried body in linen bandages soaked in resin (plant gum). Put the lungs, liver, stomach and intestines into four stone jars, called canopic jars, and seal up. Give finished mummy to dead person's relatives to be placed in a decorated coffin, and buried in a tomb.

(As recorded by the Greek traveller and scholar Herodotus. He visited Egypt around 500 BC.)

← 16.00hrs
At last, the entrance to the burial chamber! It's guarded by a false door with carvings; this let the mummy's spirit travel between the worlds of the living and the dead.

17.30hrs →
Little shabti figures shimmer in the darkness. They look just like the one Great Grandpa brought back from Egypt many years ago.

Image 2

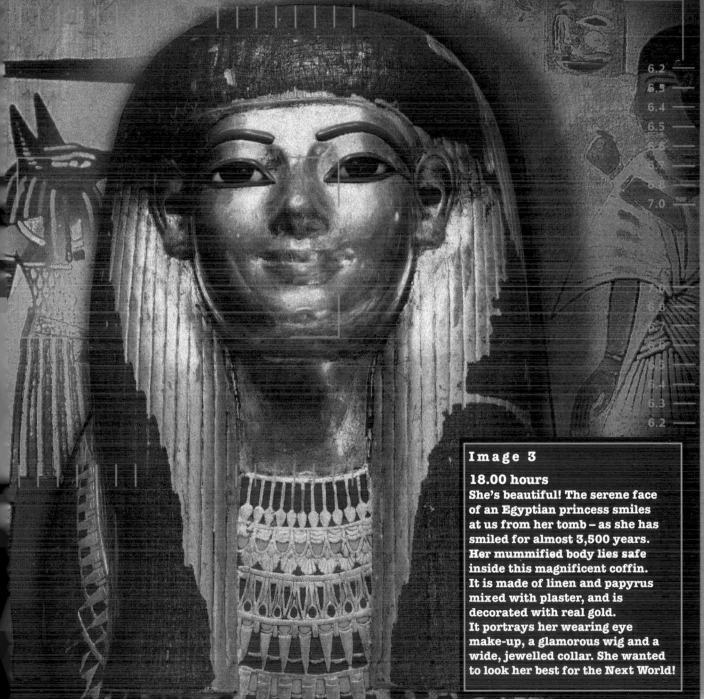

6.2
6.3
6.4
6.5
6.6
6.7
6.8
7.0

6.8

6.3
6.2

Image 3

18.00 hours
She's beautiful! The serene face of an Egyptian princess smiles at us from her tomb – as she has smiled for almost 3,500 years. Her mummified body lies safe inside this magnificent coffin. It is made of linen and papyrus mixed with plaster, and is decorated with real gold. It portrays her wearing eye make-up, a glamorous wig and a wide, jewelled collar. She wanted to look her best for the Next World!

Six months later

It's great to be back in Egypt, but it's just a quick trip this time. The Egyptian archaeologists were given extra time to excavate the tomb properly, and now Dr. Smith is taking me to visit the experts who have been investigating 'our' mummy.

Dr. Smith laughed when I asked how they would unwrap her. She said I was very old-fashioned! Archaeologists today try not to unwrap mummies, or cut them open. Instead, they use X-rays, CAT scans and endoscopes to 'see' inside the bandages, without disturbing them. X-rays of bones can tell archaeologists whether mummies were male or female, approximately how old they were when they died and even whether they were well fed.

I can't wait to see what's inside that beautiful gold coffin.

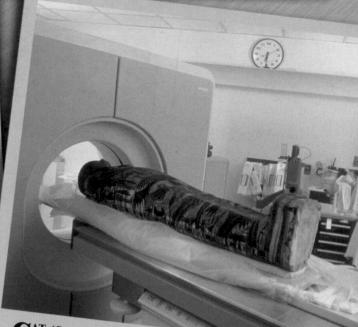

CAT (Computed Axial Tomography) scanners take pictures of cross-sections (like 'slices') through a mummy at 5 mm intervals. A special computer can then rearrange these to create 3-D pictures of the inside of the mummy, from any angle.

25th November 1935

Visited my old college friend Brown, who is digging near Cairo. Found him surrounded by tangled bits of bandage. He was busily unwrapping a mummy to get at the bones inside. Pity to see something so old destroyed in this way, but it's the only way to increase our knowledge.

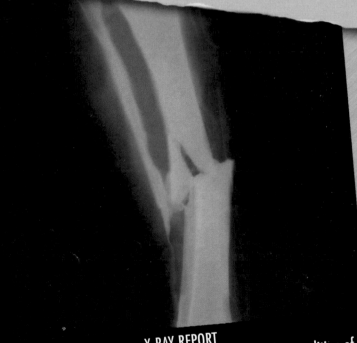

X-RAY REPORT

Malnutrition leaves distinctive scars on bones, but the condition of this mummy's bones suggests she was well nourished. The X-ray has revealed an injury too. This broken leg might have happened in a fall, but it may have been snapped by a crocodile! Many Egyptians were attacked by crocodiles as they bathed in the River Nile. They suffered horrible bites and broken bones, lost arms and legs or were even killed.

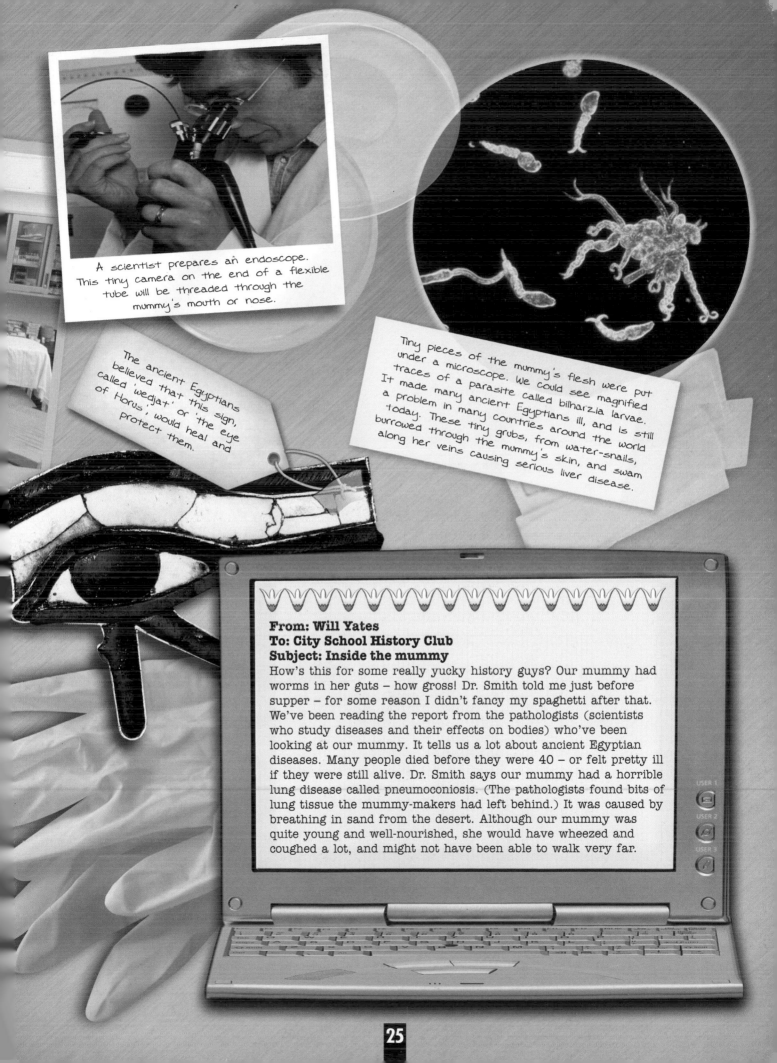

A scientist prepares an endoscope. This tiny camera on the end of a flexible tube will be threaded through the mummy's mouth or nose.

The ancient Egyptians believed that this sign, called 'wedjat' or 'the eye of Horus', would heal and protect them.

Tiny pieces of the mummy's flesh were put under a microscope. We could see magnified traces of a parasite called bilharzia larvae. It made many ancient Egyptians ill, and is still a problem in many countries around the world today. These tiny grubs, from water-snails, burrowed through the mummy's skin, and swam along her veins causing serious liver disease.

From: Will Yates
To: City School History Club
Subject: Inside the mummy

How's this for some really yucky history guys? Our mummy had worms in her guts – how gross! Dr. Smith told me just before supper – for some reason I didn't fancy my spaghetti after that. We've been reading the report from the pathologists (scientists who study diseases and their effects on bodies) who've been looking at our mummy. It tells us a lot about ancient Egyptian diseases. Many people died before they were 40 – or felt pretty ill if they were still alive. Dr. Smith says our mummy had a horrible lung disease called pneumoconiosis. (The pathologists found bits of lung tissue the mummy-makers had left behind.) It was caused by breathing in sand from the desert. Although our mummy was quite young and well-nourished, she would have wheezed and coughed a lot, and might not have been able to walk very far.

USER 1
USER 2
USER 3

In the laboratory

I've seen our mummy!
We went to the laboratory, here in Egypt, where she's being cleaned, checked and treated with chemicals. Then she will be stored in the right conditions, to make sure she doesn't decay. Dr. Smith says this is called 'conservation'. The mummy was much smaller than I thought she'd be. I was surprised to see how shrivelled and leathery she looked where the bandages had slipped away from her skin. Dr. Smith explained that a human body is 75% water. The natron salt dries up all the water, during the mummification process, so the mummy shrinks as it dries.

The conservators showed us the other objects from the tomb that they were working on too. Then they let us see the latest X-rays. And guess what, the X-rays showed she'd been stabbed. Our mummy was murdered!

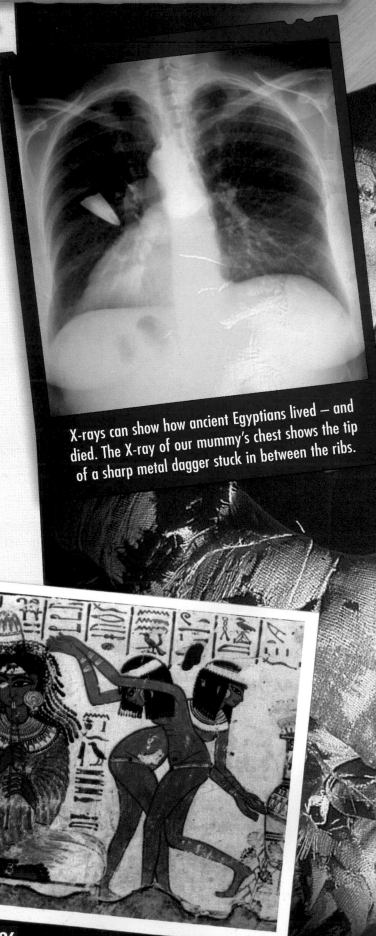

X-rays can show how ancient Egyptians lived — and died. The X-ray of our mummy's chest shows the tip of a sharp metal dagger stuck in between the ribs.

TOMB PAINTINGS
Conservation Report

Damaging salt crystals grow on tomb walls whenever they get damp, for example when the ground above a tomb is flooded. Visitors to tombs also cause harm. The moisture in their breath makes the salt crystals grow faster pushing the paintings off the walls. Air conditioning will be installed in the tomb to remove all moisture and protect the original painting, and a replica will be produced to go on display in the museum.

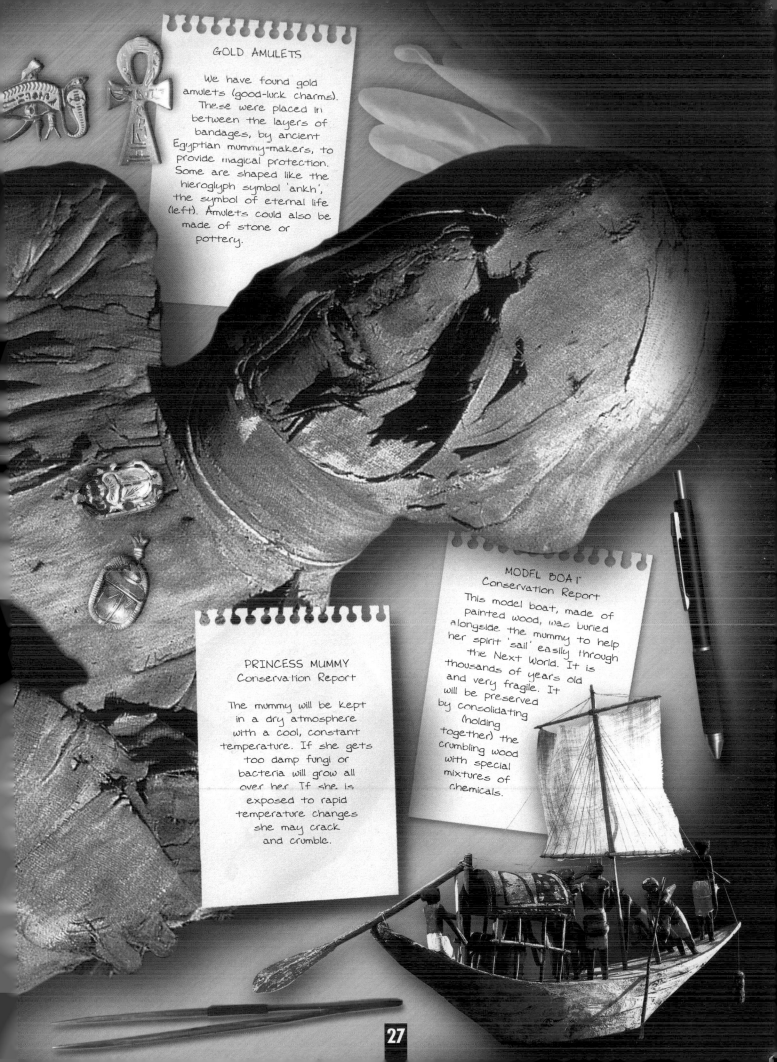

GOLD AMULETS

We have found gold amulets (good-luck charms). These were placed in between the layers of bandages, by ancient Egyptian mummy-makers, to provide magical protection. Some are shaped like the hieroglyph symbol 'ankh', the symbol of eternal life (left). Amulets could also be made of stone or pottery.

PRINCESS MUMMY
Conservation Report

The mummy will be kept in a dry atmosphere with a cool, constant temperature. If she gets too damp fungi or bacteria will grow all over her. If she is exposed to rapid temperature changes she may crack and crumble.

MODEL BOAT
Conservation Report

This model boat, made of painted wood, was buried alongside the mummy to help her spirit 'sail' easily through the Next World. It is thousands of years old and very fragile. It will be preserved by consolidating (holding together) the crumbling wood with special mixtures of chemicals.

THE PRINCESS MUMMY

Famous at last

I'm going to be on TV. A documentary (a factual TV programme) is being made about our mummy, and they want all the museum team to be in it. We went to the studio today. I told the interviewer all about Great Grandpa's travels, and Dr. Smith described our dig in Egypt.

Dr. Smith has been trying to fill in all the gaps in our mummy's life by studying history books, and by poring over documents written by ancient Egyptian scribes. The elaborate tomb and beautiful jewellery make Dr. Smith think that our mummy was a princess married to a pharaoh. She lived in a palace surrounded by beautiful gardens with musicians and dancers to entertain her (as seen in her tomb paintings). She was well nourished; so she probably ate good food like fresh fruit and vegetables, oxen and gazelles and fish caught in the Nile. But who killed her? And why was she murdered? Dr. Smith is writing a book which she says will answer these questions. I can't wait to read it!

The mummy, her coffin and a replica dagger are on display at the museum in Egypt. The TV camera crew have set-up their equipment to film the artefacts for the documentary.

THE PRINCESS MUMMY
The story of a murdered princess
Dr. Jane Smith & Dr. Mokhtar Ahmad

These great little shabti toys will go on sale in the City Museum gift shop.

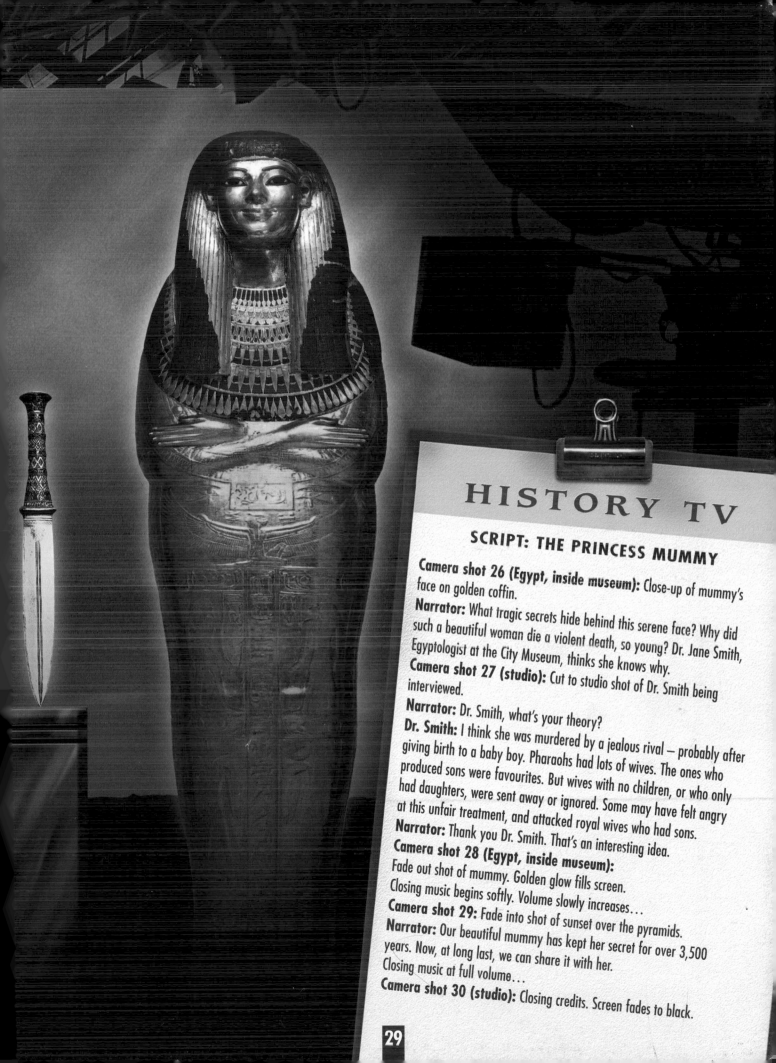

HISTORY TV

SCRIPT: THE PRINCESS MUMMY

Camera shot 26 (Egypt, inside museum): Close-up of mummy's face on golden coffin.

Narrator: What tragic secrets hide behind this serene face? Why did such a beautiful woman die a violent death, so young? Dr. Jane Smith, Egyptologist at the City Museum, thinks she knows why.

Camera shot 27 (studio): Cut to studio shot of Dr. Smith being interviewed.

Narrator: Dr. Smith, what's your theory?

Dr. Smith: I think she was murdered by a jealous rival — probably after giving birth to a baby boy. Pharaohs had lots of wives. The ones who produced sons were favourites. But wives with no children, or who only had daughters, were sent away or ignored. Some may have felt angry at this unfair treatment, and attacked royal wives who had sons.

Narrator: Thank you Dr. Smith. That's an interesting idea.

Camera shot 28 (Egypt, inside museum):
Fade out shot of mummy. Golden glow fills screen.
Closing music begins softly. Volume slowly increases…

Camera shot 29: Fade into shot of sunset over the pyramids.

Narrator: Our beautiful mummy has kept her secret for over 3,500 years. Now, at long last, we can share it with her.
Closing music at full volume…

Camera shot 30 (studio): Closing credits. Screen fades to black.

GLOSSARY

Amulets Ancient Egyptian lucky charms.

Anubis The jackal-headed ancient Egyptian god of the dead.

Archaeologist Someone who studies the past by examining the physical remains left behind.

Artefacts Objects made by humans, for example a tool or pot. Often they are the subject of an archaeological study.

Canopic jars Pottery jars used to hold the lungs, liver, intestines and stomach of a mummified person.

Conservation The scientific process of cleaning, mending and preserving ancient objects.

Curator Senior member of the staff of a museum, in charge of its collections.

Dam Large wall built to hold back the waters of a river or lake.

Demotic (writing) A simplified script (type of writing). It was used for business, scientific and religious writings.

Egyptologist A person who studies all aspects of life in ancient Egypt.

Excavation Investigation of ancient remains that are often (but not always) buried underground.

Faience A material made from crushed quartz mixed with a little ash and lime. It was used to make jewellery and decorate pottery. Often a beautiful blue-green.

Felucca Boat with a shallow hull and large sails. Feluccas are used by modern-day sailors on the River Nile.

Fertile (land) Land where crops grow very well.

Hieroglyphs Picture signs used in ancient Egyptian writing. Each sign stood for a sound, an object or an idea.

Hieratic (writing) A shorthand version of hieroglyphic script. It was used by scribes and priests for stories, letters and business contracts.

Horus The falcon or hawk-headed god of the sky. He protected each ruling pharaoh.

Kiln Oven where pottery is baked at very high temperatures.

Linen A cloth woven from the strong, woody fibres of the flax plant.

Mummification The process of preserving dead bodies. The Egyptians believed that a dead person's soul only lived for as long as their body remained unharmed.

Natron Salty crystals found in the Egyptian

desert. They absorbed moisture and were used to make mummies.

Next World According to the ancient Egyptians, a place where your spirit went after death.

Nilometer A series of steps or a tall pillar marked in bands. They were used to measure the level of River Nile floods.

Nut The ancient Egyptian goddess of the sky.

Papyrus A tall reed-like plant that grows beside the River Nile. It was used for making paper, boats and even sandals.

Pathologist A doctor or scientist who studies the bodies of dead people.

Pharaoh The ruler of ancient Egypt.

Pneumoconiosis A crippling lung disease caused by regularly breathing in an irritant mineral or particles of metal. The ancient Egyptians suffered with this disease because they breathed in sand.

Pyramid A large, pointed monument or building with a wide square base and sloping sides.

Scarab Dung beetle. For the ancient Egyptians, a sign of eternal life.

Scribe A professional writer, a sort of clerk or civil servant.

Shabti A model figure that was buried in a tomb alongside a mummy. In the next world, the shabti would carry out work on behalf of the dead person.

Sphinx Ancient monster with a human head and the body of a lion. For the ancient Egyptians the Sphinx was a symbol of royal power.

Spirit Invisible essence of a personality. Another word for 'soul'.

Stele A stone pillar with carvings.

Surveyor Expert worker who measures land.

Temple The home of a god. A large building used for worship.

Tomb Chamber where dead bodies are buried.

INDEX

t=top, b=bottom, c=centre, l=left, r=right, OFC=outside front cover, OBC=outside back cover

Alamy images: OFCl, 3b, 4tr, 5tl, 10tr, 11b, 12tr, 14tr, 14br, 16br, 20cb, 24br, 26tr, 26b. Corbis: OFCbr, 4tc, 6tr, 6-7c, 7tl, 8tr, 8bc, 8-9b, 9cr, 10-11c, 11tr, 12cr, 12-13, 15tr, 16-17c, 19cr, 23c, 26-27c, 28-29c, 29cl. Heritage Images: 9t. Popperfoto: 22tr. Science Photo Library: 22cr, 24tr, 25tl, 25tr.

Every effort has been made to trace the copyright holders, and we apologize in advance for any unintentional omissions. We would be pleased to insert the appropriate acknowledgements in any subsequent edition of this publication.

HISTORY HUNTERS

THE LOST MUMMY

A unique combination of fact and fiction, this gripping adventure story is packed with information about life and death in ancient Egypt.

Join an adventure

Somewhere in the Egyptian desert a mysterious ancient tomb is buried. Armed with just two clues to its location – a Victorian diary and an old sketch – Will Yates and the team from the City Museum are about to embark on a new expedition...

Work with experts

Be an eyewitness to the discovery of an ancient Egyptian tomb. Find out how archaeologists plan a 'dig'. Learn about the techniques and equipment they use to excavate ancient artefacts, and experience the excitement of being the first person to see a mummy that has been buried for 3,500 years!

Uncover the facts

Piece together a story from the past using evidence uncovered on the archaeological dig and scientific facts revealed by research carried out in the museum laboratory.

A fascinating and informative look at the lives of the ancient Egyptians combined with exciting factual details about the work of archaeologists.

£ 4.99

ISBN 1-86007-372-7

9 781860 073724